SPACE SYSTEMS:
PATTERNS AND CYCLES

SUN

Priyanka Das
and Heather Kissock

LIGHTBOX
openlightbox.com

LIGHTBOX

Go to **www.openlightbox.com** and enter this book's unique code.

ACCESS CODE

LBXG6653

Lightbox is an all-inclusive digital solution for the teaching and learning of curriculum topics in an original, groundbreaking way. Lightbox is based on National Curriculum Standards.

OPTIMIZED FOR

- ✓ TABLETS
- ✓ WHITEBOARDS
- ✓ COMPUTERS
- ✓ AND MUCH MORE!

STANDARD FEATURES OF LIGHTBOX

AUDIO High-quality narration using text-to-speech system

VIDEOS Embedded high-definition video clips

ACTIVITIES Printable PDFs that can be emailed and graded

WEBLINKS Curated links to external, child-safe resources

SLIDESHOWS Pictorial overviews of key concepts

INTERACTIVE MAPS Interactive maps and aerial satellite imagery

QUIZZES Ten multiple choice questions that are automatically graded and emailed for teacher assessment

KEY WORDS Matching key concepts to their definitions

VIDEOS

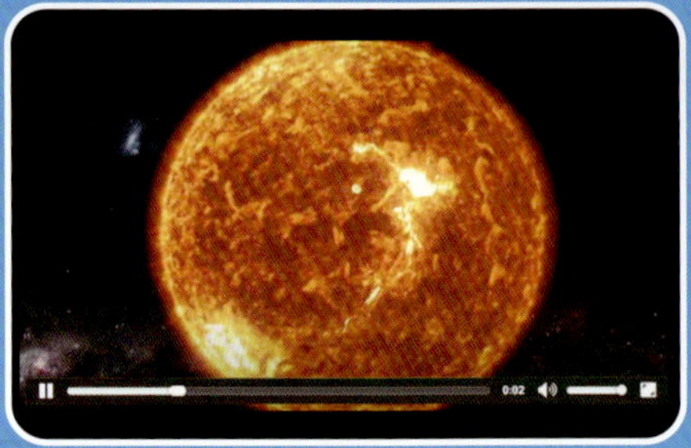

WEBLINKS

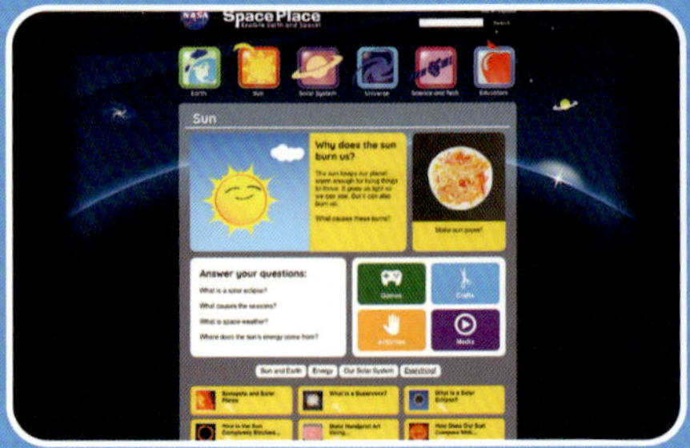

SLIDESHOWS

QUIZZES

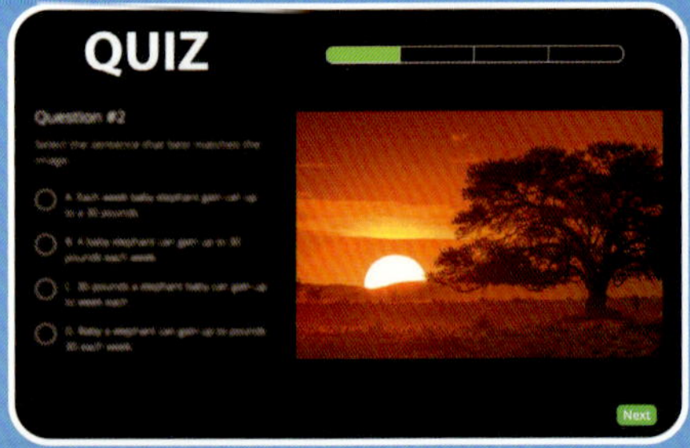

SUN

Contents

The Sun makes all life possible. Its heat and light help things live and grow.

Did you know that the Sun is a **star**? It is made up of very hot gases.

The Sun's **gravity** pulls objects toward it. One of these objects is Earth.

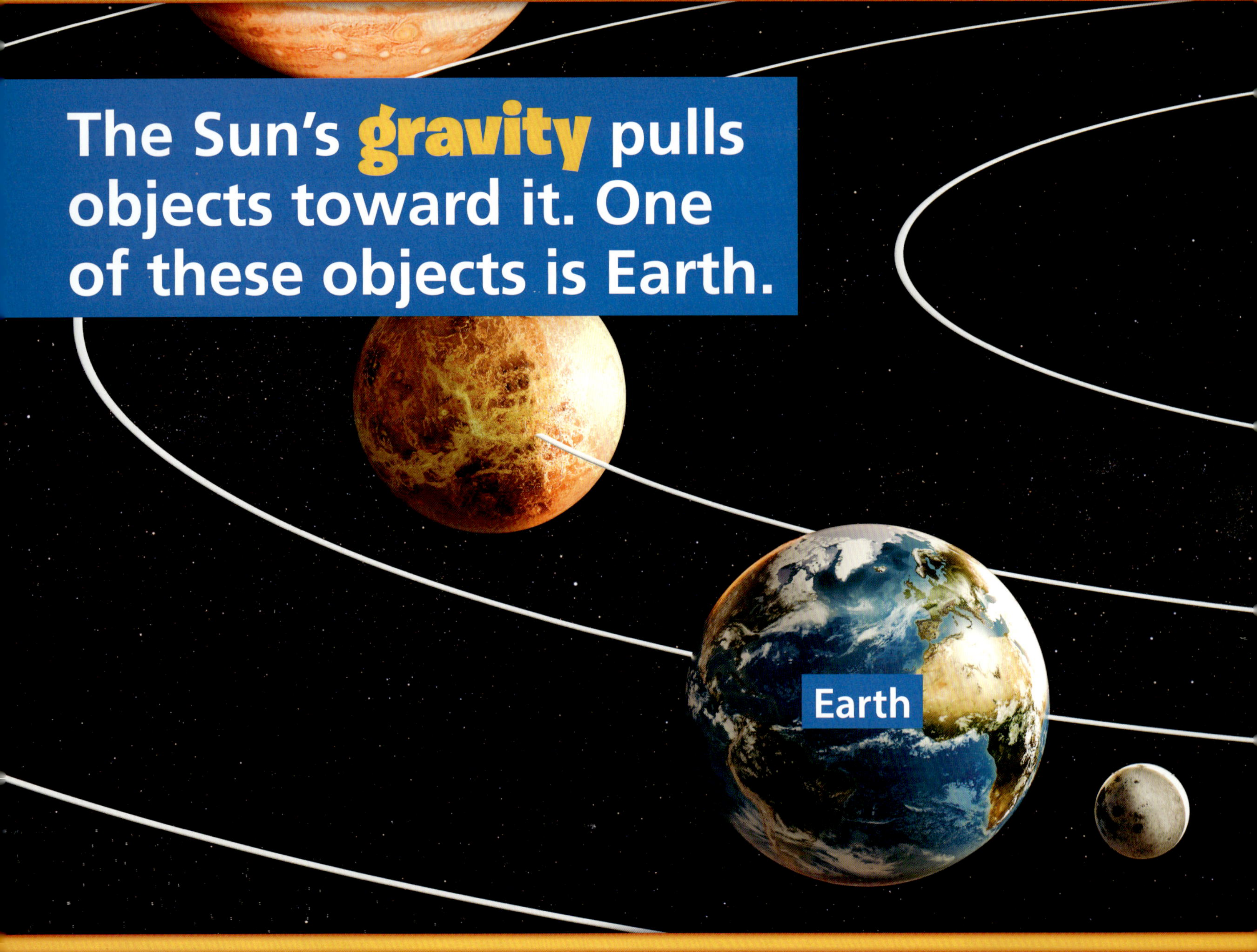

Earth travels **around** the Sun because of the Sun's gravity.

The Sun is much **larger** than Earth. It looks smaller because it is very far away.

More than **1 million** Earths could fit **inside** the Sun.

Earth receives the Sun's **energy** as light and heat. This energy gives us the **weather** and **seasons**, too.

The amount of **light** and **heat** from the Sun changes through the year.

Earth moves around the Sun in an **orbit**. Our planet also **rotates** on its axis every 24 hours.

When one half of Earth faces the Sun, the other half faces away. This gives us **day** and **night**.

The Sun shines during the day. Every morning, we first see it in the **east**. It then appears to travel across the sky.

The Sun sets in the **west**.
It cannot be seen at night.

It takes about **8 minutes** for light from the Sun to reach **Earth**.

Earth's journey around the Sun takes **365 days**, or **one year**. The seasons change during the year.

The four seasons are **summer**, **fall**, **winter**, and **spring**.

Earth leans toward the Sun. **Summer**, the hottest season, begins. It has the longest hours of daylight.

Fall comes after summer. There are fewer daylight hours.

Earth leans away from the Sun. **Winter** begins. It is the coldest season with the shortest days.

Spring follows winter. The days become longer again.

It is **dangerous** to look directly at the Sun. **Solar telescopes** help people study it. Telescopes make far-away objects look closer.

The **largest** solar telescope in the **world** sits on top of a **volcano** in **Hawai'i**.

Activity: Sunrise and Sunset

How long are days in winter? Are they longer than days in spring? You can find out by studying the sky this year. Remember, daytime lasts from sunrise to sunset.

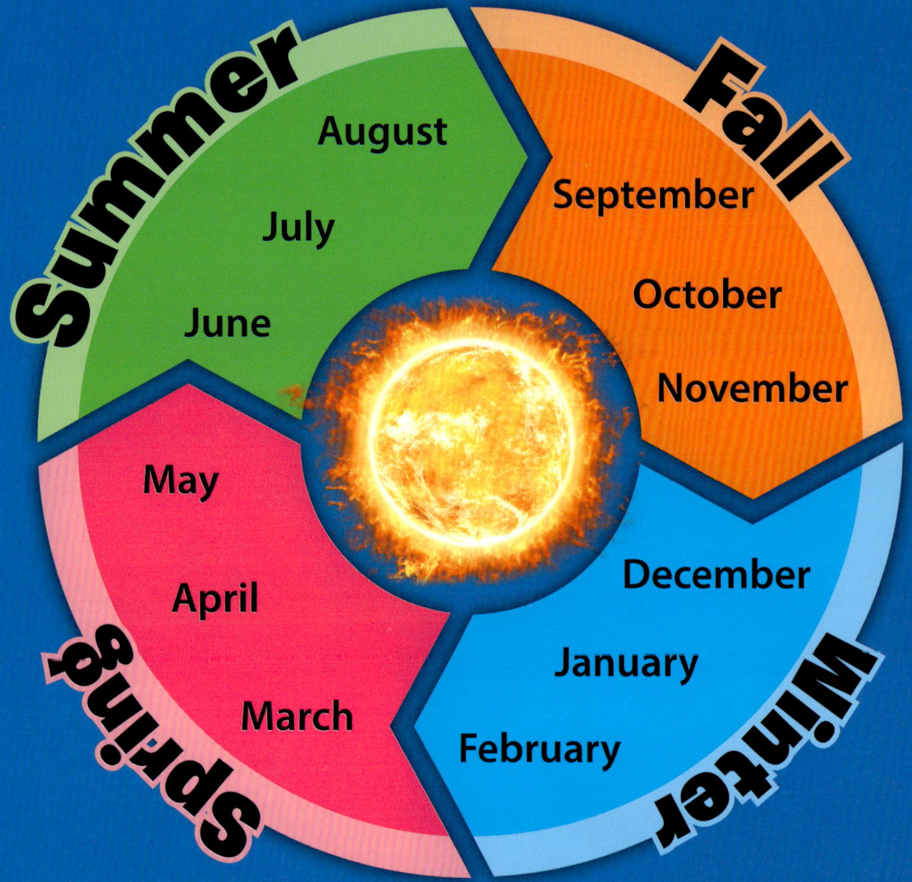

Steps

1. Put up a calendar.
2. On the first day of a month, find out what time the Sun rises. Write it down.
3. Then, write down the time that the Sun sets on the same day.
4. Do this for at least six months.

Match each month to its season. What do you notice? Are the days becoming longer or shorter?

KEY WORDS

Research has shown that as much as 65 percent of all written material published in English is made up of 300 words. These 300 words cannot be taught using pictures or learned by sounding them out. They must be recognized by sight. This book contains 80 common sight words to help young readers improve their reading fluency and comprehension. This book also teaches young readers several important content words, such as proper nouns. These words are paired with pictures to aid in learning and improve understanding.

Page	Sight Words First Appearance
4	a, all, and, did, grow, help, is, it, its, know, life, light, live, made, makes, of, that, the, things, up, very, you
6	Earth, one, these
7	around, because
9	away, could, far, looks, more, much, than
10	as, gives, this, too, us
11	changes, from, through, year
12	also, an, every, in, moves, on, our
13	day, faces, night, other, when
14	first, see, then, to, we
15	about, at, be, for, sets, takes
16	or
17	are, four
18	after, begins, comes, has, there
19	again, follows, with
20	people, study
21	world

Page	Content Words First Appearance
4	gases, heat, star, Sun
6	gravity, objects
10	energy, seasons, weather
11	amount
12	axis, hours, orbit, planet
13	half
14	east, morning, sky
15	minutes, west
16	journey
17	fall, spring, summer, winter
18	daylight
20	solar telescopes
21	Hawai'i, volcano

Published by Smartbook Media Inc.
14 Penn Plaza, 9th Floor New York, NY 10122
Website: www.openlightbox.com

Library of Congress Control Number: 2020936990

ISBN 978-1-5105-5524-2 (hardcover)
ISBN 978-1-5105-5525-9 (multi-user eBook)

Printed in Guangzhou, China
1 2 3 4 5 6 7 8 9 0 24 23 22 21 20

052020
110819

Project Coordinator: Priyanka Das
Designer: Ana María Vidal

The publisher acknowledges Alamy, Getty Images, iStock, Shutterstock, and Wikimedia as the primary image suppliers for this title.